The Monster in the Attic

Lisa Trumbauer

Illustrated by Sergi Camara

Rigby®

A Harcourt Achieve Imprint

www.Rigby.com
1-800-531-5015

"It is time to go to sleep, Jack," said Mom. "Your birthday is tomorrow."

But that night, a loud noise woke Jack up.

Boom!

Jack jumped out of bed and ran to his sister's room next door.

"Liz! I think there is a monster in the attic!" said Jack.

Jack and Liz slowly walked to the stairs.

Tap! Tap! Tap! Tap!

"The monster must have a lot of feet!"
said Jack.

Clang! Crunch!

"It sounds like the monster is eating," said Liz.

"We need to wake up Mom!" said Jack.
"OK," said Liz.

"What are you doing up?" asked Mom.

"There is a monster in the attic," said Jack.

Mom smiled.
"Come with me," she said.

Mom took the children up to the attic.
She opened the attic door.

Jack and Liz saw something move.
"That's not a monster," said Liz.

"It's a puppy!" said Jack.
"Happy birthday, Jack!" said Dad.

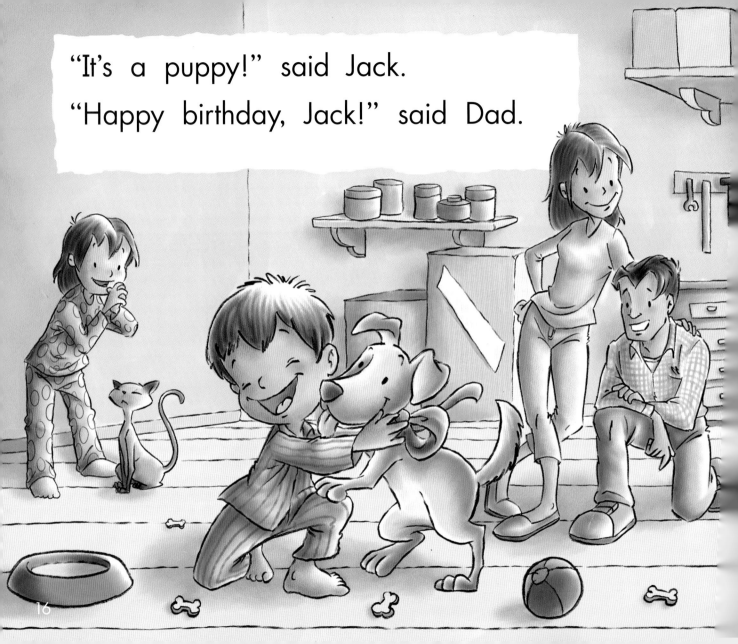